IRISH Dad JOKES

Des MacHale

IRISH Dad JOKES

MERCIER PRESS

IRISH PUBLISHER – IRISH STORY

MERCIER PRESS

Cork

www.mercierpress.ie

© Des MacHale, 2024

ISBN: 978 1 78117 946 8

A CIP record for this title is available from the British Library

Introduction

When I was a child, many years ago, my father Jack McHale, told me an endless stream of 'groan' jokes and he may have been one of the first people to exploit this now very popular genre of dad jokes, long before the name was invented. He loved wordplay, puns and clever quips, and one of the first I remember was when I asked him for money because I had been a good boy, he replied, 'You should be like your father, good for nothing'. Of course, I thought his jokes were hilarious, and that is the whole point; children (he hated the word 'kids' which he said would have implied that he was a goat!) always regard their dads' jokes as very funny indeed and as they enter their teens and adulthood keep up the pretence that they still do. This is a much-neglected part of the bonding and love between father and children and long may it continue. I now possess possibly the largest collection of jokes in the world, but I still fondly remember the ones my dad first told me, and I am sure he guided me in the direction of being a joke-collector and the author of over fifty jokebooks. This collection of *Irish Dad Jokes* is dedicated to him with much love.

One yellow line on the road means no parking
at all.
Two yellow lines mean no parking at all, at all.

☘

Teacher to new boy in Junior Infants: And what
is your name?
Tom, miss.
No, your name is not Tom, it is Thomas.
And now, what is your name, next little boy?
Jackass, miss.

☘

What country has the biggest city in the world?
Ireland, because its capital is always Dublin.

☘

I have a dog who is really clever at arithmetic.
When I ask him what three minus three is, he
says nothing.

☘

Waiter: Your bill, sir.
Diner: I'm not Bill, I'm Mick.

🍀

Irish people like camping because the fun is intense.

🍀

What did Saint Patrick say when he was driving the snakes out of Ireland?
Are ye all right in the back there lads?

🍀

If a farmer raises corn in the dry season and beef cattle all the year round, what does he raise in the rainy season?
An umbrella.

🍀

Hotel guest: I'd like you to give me a room and a bath please.

Clerk: I can give you a room, but you will have to take your own bath, madam.

A little girl went into a butcher's shop in Cork with a note from her mother:
Dear butcher, please give Mary a twenty-euro leg of lamb as I am in bed with a new-born baby and three pork chops.

What kind of monster gets up your nose?
A bogeyman.

How do you make a slow horse fast?
Don't feed him any hay.

Our next-door neighbours are keeping pigs.
We just got wind of it yesterday.

Client: Is it true that you charge 500 euro to answer just three questions?
Lawyer: That is correct.
Client: Isn't that very expensive?
Lawyer: Yes it is. Now what is your third question?

Mother Bear and Father Bear had a Baby Bear who was completely bald.
They called him Fred. Because he was Fred Bear.

Where do frogs play football?
At Croak Park.

Irish bees are going on strike. They are looking for shorter flowers and more honey.

A sausage and a rasher were being cooked
together in a frying pan.
Said the sausage, 'It's pretty hot in here'.
'Wow', said the rasher, 'I've never heard a
talking sausage before'.

What does RTE stand for?
Really Terrible Entertainment.

'Always learn to cut your fingernails with your
left hand, my son', my old daddy used to say, 'in
case you lose your right hand'.

We should value Venetian blinds, because
without them it would be curtains for all of us.

What is the best way to catch a rabbit?
Pour salt on its tail (my dad's favourite).

What is the best way to get down from an elephant?
You don't get down from an elephant—you get down from a duck.

A man was seriously injured after being hit by a tomato. How come?
The tomato was in a tin.

Why did the rubber chicken cross the road?
To stretch her legs.

Why did the cow jump over the moon?
Because the farmer's hands were very, very cold.

A woman was swimming around in shark-infested waters.
But she survived because all of the sharks were man-eaters.

What time is it if your clock strikes thirteen?
Time to buy a new clock.

This fellow was running races all his life with no success. Finally, he won a race and said, 'I'm first at last—I was always behind before'.

An Irishman has just invented a silent alarm clock for people who like to sleep a lot. He has been awarded the no bell prize.

'Banjaxed' is Irish for 'the ladies' toilet is out of order'.

🍀

What is another name for dad's jokes?
Popcorn!

🍀

Quiz Master: Who was the first woman in the world?
Contestant: I don't know—give me a clue.
Quiz Master: I shouldn't really, but it has something to do with an apple.
Contestant: Granny Smith.

🍀

Teacher: A comet is a type of star with a tail. Can anyone name a comet for me?
Pupil: Mickey Mouse.

Have you heard about the Irish farmer who won the Nobel Prize for Agriculture?
He was simply a man out standing in his field.

What is the smallest pole in the world?
A tadpole.

My wife's teeth are like stars.
They come out every night.

This fellow goes to the doctor complaining of severe pains in his feet.
So the doctor examines him and says, 'I see the problem. You've got your shoes on the wrong feet.'
'But doc,' said the man, 'I haven't got any other feet.'

Where do fish keep their money?
In a river bank—in the current account.

A man went fishing but all he caught was a glove.
But it was filled with fish fingers.

A little lad of six years of age sat on his
grandad's knee and asked him, 'Grandad, were
you in the Ark with Noah?'
'No', he smiled, 'I was not'.
'Then how come you weren't drowned?' asked
the little lad.

What Irish city can float?
Cork.

Mary: Why is your nose all red and swollen?
Tom: Because I smelled a brose.
Mary: But there is no b in rose.
Tom: There was in this one.

🍀

I was at a very sad wedding once. Even the cake was in tiers.

🍀

Which Irish county can be used to walk a dog?
Laois.

🍀

Teacher: If Tom gave you two apples and Bill gave you three apples, how many apples would you have?
Mary: Six apples, Miss.
Teacher: But 2 + 3 = 5, Mary.
Mary: I know that Miss, but I have an apple already.

What is the best Irish butter?
A goat.

Two lions escaped from Fota Zoo Park and were walking down Patrick Street in Cork City. One of them said to the other, 'Very quiet for a Saturday afternoon, isn't it?'

Dentist: You have some cavity, some cavity, some cavity.
Patient: There is no need to repeat it.
Dentist: I wasn't repeating it, that was an echo.

Have you heard about the woman who moved from Dublin to Galway to be nearer her son who was in New York?

🍀

Never get involved with a tennis player—love means nothing to them.

🍀

You have just damaged my Stradivarius violin. It is over four hundred years old.
Thank goodness it wasn't a new one.

🍀

What a football match that was. The referee was wearing spectacles over his contact lenses.

🍀

When playing cards, always make sure the other players are playing the cards you dealt them.

🍀

What is cows' favourite form of entertainment?
Moosicals!

🍀

This fellow had a car with wooden seats,
wooden wheels and a wooden engine.
It wouldn't go!

🍀

Why did the golfer wear two pairs of trousers?
In case he got a hole in one.

🍀

Little boy: Mum, I can do something my
teacher cannot do.
Mum: Well done, son, what is it?
Little boy: Read my handwriting.

🍀

Lady in shoe shop: I'd like some crocodile shoes
please.
Sales assistant: Certainly madam. What size
does your crocodile take?

🍀

A sheep's girlfriend left him and he began to sing sad songs, starting with 'I'll never find another ewe'.

What do you call a man with a toilet on his head? John.
And what do you call a girl with two toilets on her head? Lulu.

A woman was getting a haircut when she noticed that the hairdresser's hands were very dirty.
The hairdresser explained that nobody had been in for a shampoo yet.

Noah was the world's first great financier because he floated alone when the whole world was in liquidation.

What three keys can't you put in your pocket?
A donkey, a monkey and a turkey.

Spell hungry horse with just three letters.
MTGG.

Why was six afraid?
Because seven ate nine.

What did the boy say when he saw three holes in the ground?
Well, well, well.

Where do all unemployed Irish politicians hang out?
Dole Eireann.

If every car in the country was pink, then Ireland would be a pink car nation.

I am getting rid of my old damaged vacuum cleaner. Well, it is better than having it lying round the house gathering dust.

Nature always compensates for your deficiencies.
If you have poor eyesight, you will have good hearing.
If you are bald, you can grow a beard.
And if one of your legs is a bit short, the other one will always be a bit longer.

Two cannibals were eating a clown.
One said to the other, 'Does he taste funny to you?'

If you want to start a fire by rubbing two sticks together, make sure that one of the sticks is a match.

Diner: I've been waiting here for twenty-five minutes.
Waiter: That's nothing sir, I've been waiting here for twenty-five years.

This guy saw an ad on the telly:
When walking on the road stay safe by wearing something white.
So he bought a white coat, a white hat and white wellies.
He got run over by a snowplough.

Which Irish town contains the most
ambulances?
Nen-agh, Nen-agh, Nen-agh.

🍀

People do not swim in Dublin Bay—they are
merely going through the motions.

🍀

Billy: I've just swallowed a fishbone.
Milly: Are you choking?
Billy: No, I'm serious.

🍀

Husband: I dreamed last night I was kicked by
a horse.
Wife: That must have been a nightmare.

🍀

Sherlock Holmes: My dear Watson, you are
wearing your pink polka-dot underpants again.

Watson: That is fantastic, Holmes. How on earth did you deduce that?
Holmes: You've forgotten to put your trousers on.

🍀

Lawyer to dentist: Do you promise to pull the tooth, the whole tooth, and nothing but the truth?

🍀

This fellow opened his fridge door and found a rabbit sitting inside.
'What are you doing in my fridge?' he asked angrily.
'This is a Westinghouse, is it not?' said the rabbit.
'Yes, it is', said the fellow, 'but what has that got to do with it?'
'Well, I am a wabbit, and I'm westing'.

🍀

What happened to the guy who fell through a window?
He got a pane in the neck.

What is the best place to put your hands when singing?
How about over your mouth?

You can beat an egg, you can beat a hasty retreat, but you cannot beat a broken drum.

I was the most famous boy in my class in school. I went down in history.

Why do we think Santa Claus may be Irish?
In the average house there are eight windows and two doors, but he always comes down the chimney.

What question can you never answer with the word 'Yes'?
Are you asleep?

How many sides does a circle have?
Two—the inside and the outside.

What is the last thing you take off before you go to bed at night?
Your feet off the floor.

What do rabbits do after they get married?
They go on bunnymoon.

Children really brighten up your house—they never switch the lights off.

Why do polar bears have white fur coats?
They'd look funny in anoraks.

This young couple decided to call their baby
Bill, because he was due at the end of the
month.

What do you stuff a parrot with?
Pollyfilla.

What is frogs' favourite drink?
Croak-a-cola.

What did the mayonnaise say to the fridge?
Keep that door shut, I'm dressing.

Diner: Waiter, do I have to sit here all night until I starve?
No sir, we close at ten o'clock.

🍀

Have you heard about the clown who swallowed the OXO cube?
He made a laughing stock of himself.

🍀

If you are bald, console yourself that you always come out on top.

🍀

Two astronauts were in a space capsule together circling the earth. One of them went on a space walk
When he got back, he knocked loudly on the door.
'Who's there?' said the other astronaut.

🍀

Why is it dangerous to take a nap in a railway station?
Because the train always runs over sleepers.

Three peanuts were walking down the street together.
One of them was assaulted.

Which Irish county has the saddest hills?
County Down with its Mountains of Mourne.

I was going to get my brother-in-law a book for his birthday, but he has a book already.

If you have a referee in football, an umpire in cricket, what do you have in bowls?
Goldfish.

What do you call a judge with no thumbs?
Justice Fingers.

An Irish scientist has just come up with a fantastic new invention for looking through walls.
It's called a window.

What do elephants have that no other animals have?
Baby elephants!

What type of meringues can you never throw away?
Boomeringues!

What is the smallest pole in the world?
A tadpole.

What is the biggest ant in the world?
An elephant.
What is the biggest mouse in the world?
A hippopotamouse.

If your dog gets sick, where do you take it? To
the dogtor.
If your horse gets sick, where do you take it? To
horspital.
What do you give a sick ant? Antibiotics.
And if your cat gets sick where do you take it?
To the vet, of course.

What type of thief steals meat?
A beef burglar.

A fellow asked me what I would do if I was in
his shoes.

I said I would polish them.

Doctor, I feel like a snooker ball.
Go to the head of the queue immediately.

Why was a carpenter very annoyed when he hit a nail?
It was his fingernail.

How do you stop a fish from smelling?
Cut off its nose.

What is the best way to keep milk fresh?
Leave it in the cow.

What is the quickest way to contact a fish?
Drop it a line.

🍀

Who is the most reliable guy in a hospital?
The ultrasound man.
And who fills in for him at weekends?
The hip replacement guy.

🍀

This Irish wife said to her husband, 'You never tell me you love me'.
He replied, 'When we got married thirty-five years ago, I told you I loved you and if there is ever any change in that situation, you will be the first to know'.

🍀

This fellow went into the kitchen in a monastery and saw the cook preparing potatoes for dinner.
'Excuse me,' he asked him, 'are you the friar?'
'No, I'm the chip monk'.

🍀

If you need to wear a wig, always wear a wig with a big hole on the top, so nobody will know you are wearing a wig.

🍀

Help save the environment—always keep your spent lightbulbs for use in photographic darkrooms.

🍀

How can you distinguish between a weasel and a stoat?
A weasel is weasely recognised, whereas a stoat is stoately different.

🍀

What does every man overlook?
His nose.

🍀

How many ears did Davy Crockett have?
Three—a left ear, a right ear, and a wild front ear.

Why do bees hum?
Because they've forgotten the words.

Which of Santa's reindeers was a girl?
Olive the other reindeer.

What famous Irish writer used to hold up walls?
James Joist.

You never need feel hungry when on the beach.
You can always eat the sand which is there.

Why was the little ice cream sad?
Because its mother had been a wafer so long.

I bought this fantastic hearing aid and three days later I heard from my uncle in Australia.

What do you call a deer with no eyes?
No eye deer.
And what do you call a dead deer with no eyes?
Still no eye deer.

How do you make a bandstand?
Hide all their chairs.

Why do people become bakers?
Because they need the dough.

My dog's got no nose.
How does he smell?
Terrible!

Ironmonger, have you got four-inch nails?
Yes, sir.
Well, scratch my back.

How does an Eskimo build his house?
'E glues it together.

Teacher: Can you tell me what nationality
Napoleon was?
Billy: Course I can.

Should you stir your tea with your left hand or
your right hand?
Neither—you should use a spoon.

Teacher: Can you give me a sentence containing the words 'defence', 'defeat' and 'detail'?
Mickey: When a horse jumps defence, defeat go over before detail.

🍀

Who wears the biggest hat in Dail Eireann?
The TD with the biggest head.

🍀

Teacher: Where is Timbucktu?
Bridget: Midway between Timbuckone and Timbuckthree.

🍀

Three ducks were flying over Belfast.
The first duck went, 'Quack'.
The second duck went, 'Quack'.
The third duck went, 'Look, I'm goin' as quack as I can'.

🍀

What happens if a frog is illegally parked?
He gets toad away.

🍀

How do you make antifreeze?
Hide her woollen pyjamas.

🍀

What famous painter had two toilets in his house?
Two loos Lautrec.

🍀

What do you call a camel with three humps?
Humphrey.
And what do you call a camel with no humps?
Humpfree.

🍀

Billy: I think my teacher is in love with me.
Mother: What makes you think that?
Billy: She is always putting kisses on my homework.

Why was Henry the Eighth a bad-mannered king?
Because he married his wives first and axed
them afterwards.

What did the Spanish farmer say to his hens?
Ole!

How do you treat a sick pig?
Put it in the hambulance and cover it in oinkment.

What did the octopus give her husband as a
Christmas present?
Four pairs of socks.

What is the best way to make money?
Crumple a fifty euro note and you will find it in
creases.

What did the stream say when the elephant sat in it?
Well, I'll be damned!

What is the world's biggest structure made of fruit?
The Grape wall of China.

Teacher: If the Russian Emperor was called the Czar and the Empress was called the Czarina, what were their children called?
Billy: Czardines, miss.

Mum and Dad and Mickey were at the railway station waiting for a train.
'Here she comes,' said Mum.
'Here it comes,' said Dad.
'Here he comes,' said Mickey.

Who was correct?
Mickey, because it was a mail train.

Why is a rabbit's nose always shiny?
Because its powder puff is at the wrong end.

This fellow was feeling lonely and wanted
someone to talk to, so he went to a pet shop
and bought a parrot, but after a week the parrot
hadn't said a single word. So he went back to
the shop and complained.
'Buy him a little mirror for his cage', advised
the pet shop owner, 'and he will think there
is another parrot with him and begin to talk'.
So the guy did, but not a word from the
parrot.
Next time the pet shop owner advised him to buy
an exercise ladder as a speech aid, but no success.
And so it went on—toys and artefacts galore for
the cage, but not a word from the parrot.

Then one day the fellow went into the pet shop and told the owner that the parrot was dead.

'Did he say anything before he passed away?' asked the pet shop owner.

'Yes', said the fellow, 'just before he died he said, do they sell any food in that shop?'

The price of meat these days! Venison's dear isn't it?

What are Santa's elves called?
Subordinate clauses.

What did the zero say to the eight?
Nice belt man!

Why are there so few jokes about pencils?
Because most of them have no point.

🍀

Why do Claremen always part their hair in the middle?
So they will be evenly balanced when riding a bicycle.

🍀

Why are elephants such poor dancers?
Because they have two left feet.

🍀

Why do people buy such big televisions?
Why don't they just sit nearer the set?

🍀

Don't ever go to a trade union dentist.
It is a case of 'one out, all out'.

🍀

What is the best use of pigskin?
For holding the pig together.

What is the easiest way to become a millionaire on the stock exchange?
Start out as a billionaire.

Everyone laughed when I sat down to play the piano.
Why was that?
Somebody had taken away the piano stool.

What do you call an Irishman buried in a bog for a thousand years?
Pete.

A little Dublin lad was asked by his teacher to use the word 'bewitches' in a sentence.

He said, 'You go on ahead and I'll bewitches in a minute'.

🍀

Farmer: Everything I have I owe to dung. The whole success of my farm is due to dung. Dung is the basis of all my prosperity.

Daughter: Mother, could you get him to say 'fertilizer' instead of 'dung'?

Mother: Look love, it took me twenty years to get him to call it dung.

🍀

What do you get if you cross the Atlantic with the *Titanic*?

Half way.

🍀

The insects were playing football against the elephants and at the interval the elephants were leading by twenty goals to nil.

But for the second half, the insects brought on their star sub, a centipede, who scored twenty-two goals and the insects won the match.

In the post-match interview, the insects' manager was asked why he had not brought on his supersub earlier.

'Well', he replied, 'It takes him nearly an hour to get his boots on'.

🍀

What do you get if you walk under a cow?
A pat on the head.

🍀

What is lower with a head than without one?
A pillow.

🍀

If your nose runs and your feet smell, maybe you are built upside down.

🍀

Teacher: If five men build a wall in eight hours, how long will it take seven men to build the wall?
Billy: There is no need—the wall is already built.

What can go up a chimney down, but can't go down a chimney up?
An umbrella.

What grows bigger the more you take away?
A hole.

This fellow went to a dentist and was shocked to find out that it would cost a hundred euro to have a tooth extracted.
'Look', said the fellow, 'Here's ten euro—just loosen it a bit'.

What is the longest word in the English language?
Smiles—because there is a mile between the first letter and the last.

What happens if you swallow some Scrabble tiles?
You have a very painful vowel movement.

What do you call an Italian with a rubber toe?
Roberto.

What did W. B. Yeats say when he borrowed £20 from George Russell?
AEIOU.

What do you call a Cork parachutist?
Condescending.

What is worse than a giraffe with a sore throat?
An elephant with a runny nose or a hippo with chapped lips.
(Or maybe a centipede with sore feet).

What is the Irish for Brexit?
Sasamach.

What do you call a Mayoman with an All-Ireland medal?
An antique dealer.

What is the Irish for a relapse of measles?
A rash aris.

How do you start a race for teddy bears?

Ready teddy go.

🍀

My kids get all their brains from their mother.
They have to, because I've still got mine.

🍀

Níl aon thóin tinn mar do thóin tinn féin.

🍀

What is the biggest moth in the world?
A mam-moth.
And what is the biggest ant in the world?
A gi-ant'

🍀

How does a monkey make toast?
He puts it under the gorilla.

🍀

What is down even when it is up in the air?
A feather.

What is the best way to remove paint?
Sit down on it before it is dry.

What did the mathematician say when his
parrot escaped?
Polygon.

Why do I call my newt Tiny?
Because he's my newt.

What do you get if you cross a zebra with a whale?
A traffic jam.

Who didn't invent the aeroplane?
The Wrong Brothers.

I took my mother-in-law to the Chamber of Horrors in Madame Tussaud's.
The attendant said, 'Keep her moving sir, we're stocktaking'.

🍀

This farmer was on the train form Cork to Limerick for the first time.
So he hands the ticket clerk his money and is told, 'Change at Limerick Junction'.
'I'll have my change right now, if you don't mind', he retorted.

🍀

Noxious tourist: Could you recommend a really good port?
Grumpy barman: How about Rosslare?

🍀

Diner: This egg you served me is gone off.
Waitress: Don't blame me sir, I only laid the table.

✤

Billy: I took my dog to the vet to be neutered.
Mickey: Was he mad?
Billy: Mad? He was furious.

✤

Have you heard about the girl who drowned in a bowl of muesli?
A strong currant pulled her under.

✤

Baby snake: Mummy, are we a poisonous variety of snake?
Mummy snake: No son, we are not.
Baby snake: Thank goodness for that because I've just bitten my tongue.

✤

What is black and white and red all over?
A newspaper
OR a sunburned zebra

OR an embarrassed nun
OR a skunk with nappy rash.

🍀

How do you make a witch scratch?
Take away her w.

🍀

The best way to cross a field with a wild bull in it is to carry a torch.
But it all depends on how fast you carry it.

🍀

A lady went into a pet shop to buy a new coat for her dog for its birthday. The man in the shop said, 'Why not bring the dog in for a fitting, madam?'
'I can't do that', she replied, 'because I want it to be a surprise'.

🍀

Dad: Have you heard my last joke?
Billy: I certainly hope so.

🍀

Patient to Doctor: I've been having a strange dream that I am a fish.
Doctor: Don't worry, lots of people have dreams like that.
Patient: But I can't swim.

🍀

The job advert said, 'Responsible person wanted', so I decided to apply because I had been responsible for lots of things in my previous jobs.

🍀

Why does the Pope have twelve cats?
Because he's catholic.

🍀

Mickey: I sprained my ankle.
Teacher: Another lame excuse.

Why shouldn't you use washable wallpaper?
It gets stolen from the clothesline.

What do you call a Russian gardener who reads Scottish novels?
Ivanhoe.

This woman went into a Chinese restaurant and when her order arrived she lifted the lid and saw two little eyes staring out at her. So she called the waiter and complained.
'Ah', said the waiter, 'That is the peeking duck'.

Another guy in a Chinese restaurant said to the waiter, 'This chicken is rubbery'.
'Thank you very much, sir', said the waiter.

Why was the chicken in a plastic bag hanging from the cathedral?
It was the lunch pack of Notre Dame.

Why was the butterfly refused admission to the dance?
Because it was a moth ball!

Why did the football manager call his striker Cinderella?
Because he ran away from the ball.

I have every disease in the book except hypochondria.

Teacher: Can you give me two pronouns?

Billy: Who? Me?

What Irish town is populated with artificial people?
Clones.

I saw a sign which said No Access but I ignored
it because I have Mastercard.

I got this very strange email last year about
reading maps backwards.
I think it was spam.

Two fellows were on a bus in Waterford and
one says to the other,
'Are you reading that newspaper you're sitting
on, Mick?'
'I am Paddy', said Mick. So he stands up, turns

over a page of the newspaper and sits down on it again.

🍀

Patient: I cannot remember anything from one moment to the next.
Doctor: How long has this been going on?
Patient: How long has what been going on?

🍀

Customer: Cashew.
Shop assistant: Bless you.

🍀

I'm thinking of giving up stamp collecting.
Philately will get you nowhere.

🍀

Divorce is a bit like algebra. Sometimes you look at your X and wonder Y.

🍀

Who wrote Great Eggspectations?
Charles Chickens.

🍀

Why can't cars play football?
They have only one boot.

🍀

What is the maximum number of baked beans
you should eat?
Two hundred and thirty-nine.

🍀

Doctor, doctor, I keep thinking I'm a moth.
Why have you come to see me?
Well, the light was on in your surgery.

🍀

I have just won a million in the Lottery but
I don't know what to do with all the begging
letters. I think I'll just keep sending them out.

🍀

There is a new book about how to save on medical expenses when having an operation. It is called SUTURE SELF.

🍀

There is a huge December sale on at the camping store. It is the winter of our discount tent.

🍀

FINE FOR PARKING HERE—they shouldn't display such misleading notices.

🍀

What do you call a polar bear in the Sahara Desert?
Lost!

🍀

What do you call a woman with a posh bathroom who lives in Dublin?
Bidet Mulligan.

Billy: Does your watch tell the time?
Milly: No, you have to look at it.

In what Irish county is our mother?
Armagh.

My girlfriend is a twin.
How do you tell them apart?
Her brother has a moustache.

Who is always looking for better and faster numbers?
An anaesthetist.

This guy went into a deli with a huge salmon under his arm.

'Do you sell fish cakes?' he asked the girl behind the counter.

'Yes we do sir,' she replied.

'Well thank goodness for that, because it's his birthday today'.

🍀

'Twas in a café that they met
Romeo and Juliet
He had no cash to pay the debt
So Romeowed what Juliet.

🍀

Absolute zero rules OK

🍀

A shark can swim faster than I can, but I can run faster than a shark.

So in a triathlon, I reckon it would come down to whichever of us is quicker on the bicycle.

🍀

In Ireland it is no longer possible to spend a penny.

You have to euronate.

🍀

I went for a week's holiday in Ballybunion and it rained only twice.
The first time for three days and the second time for four days.

🍀

Waiter, I don't like all those flies in my soup.
Well eat all the ones you do like sir and move the others to the side of the bowl.

🍀

Which burns longer, a wax candle or a tallow candle?
Neither, all candles burn shorter.

🍀

Irish newspaper advert: Eat at Mac's Restaurant and you'll never eat anywhere else again.

What is the oldest and best known four-man American rock group?
Mount Rushmore.

What did Liam say when he dropped three ice creams?
A cone is a cone is a cone.

What does an Irish pig do when it escapes?
It runs amok.

Why does a train never sit down?
Because it's got a tender behind.

Irish restaurant sign: Try our curry. You'll never get better.

What Irish town can you buy in a fish and chip shop?
Tubbercurry.

What is a ballbearing mousetrap?
A tomcat.

What grows down as it grows up?
A duck.

This guy asked his wife what she would like for Christmas.
She said, 'Anything you like as long as it has diamonds in it'.
So he bought her a pack of playing cards.

Little Liam was standing at the side of the road for over an hour and a policeman asked him what he was doing.

'Well', he told him, 'My mother told me not to cross the road until I saw a zebra crossing, so I'm waiting and waiting and waiting'.

🍀

At Cork airport a lady was boarding a flight for Spain. In a large plastic bag she was carrying a portable television set as hand luggage.

'Why do you have that with you madam?' an official asked her.

'I don't want to miss Fair City while I'm away,' she replied.

'But they don't show Fair City on Spanish TV,' he told her.

'And that's why I'm taking my own set with me,' she smiled back at him.

🍀

This Mayo farmer bought a new mobile phone and the first place he took it with him was to the bog cutting turf. After a few minutes there, the phone rang.
'How the hell did they know I was here?' he said to himself.

An old fellow from Donegal was in hospital for the first time.
On his first morning in the ward, a nurse asked him if he would like a bedpan.
'Do I have to cook my own breakfast?' he asked.

A drummer had twin daughters. He called them Anna One, Anna Two.

What did one strawberry say to the other?
If we hadn't shared the same bed, we wouldn't be in this jam now.

The toilet has been stolen from our local Garda barracks.
The Gardaí say they have nothing to go on.

Two guys arrived at my front door and asked me what sort of bread I ate.
When I said white, they said I should be eating brown bread.
I think they were Hovis Witnesses.

Who came up with the idea of a toilet brush?
That thing hurts!

Mickey: Could I have a bar of soap. please?
Chemist: Would you like it scented, sir?
Mickey: No, I'll take it with me.

Dogs can't operate MRI machines but cats can.

Why was the little Egyptian boy confused?
Because his daddy was a mummy.

Have you heard about the guy who stayed up all
night wondering where the sun had gone to?
It finally dawned on him.

Knock, knock.
Who's there?
Irish stew.
Irish stew who?
Irish stew in the name of the law.

I ordered a chicken and an egg from Amazon in separate transactions.
That should decide it once and for all.

🍀

Why do oysters never share?
Because they are shellfish.

🍀

Have you heard about the insomniac agnostic dyslexic?
He stayed awake all night wondering if there was a dog.

🍀

Why did Mona Lisa go to jail?
Because she was framed.

🍀

My girlfriend hates me because she thinks I have no sense of direction.
So I packed my bags and right.

Two moonmen landed on Earth and one said to the other,
'You'll like this place. It's got atmosphere'.

What is a Belgian kiss?
Like a French kiss only more Flemish.

How do we know that carrots are good for your eyesight?
Well, have you ever seen a rabbit with glasses?

How can tell the difference between a can of mushroom soup and a can of elephant soup?
If there's not mushroom inside, then it's probably a can of elephant soup.

At a recital a seasoned soprano sang 'The Banks of my Own Lovely Lee', and there was a little old man sitting in the corner crying his eyes out. 'Are you a Corkman, sir?' she asked him tenderly.

'No madam,' he replied, 'I am a musician'.

Certain violinists should play the instrument solo.

So low that other people cannot hear it.

I'm filthy stinking rich—well, two out of three isn't bad.

What is the best cure for water on the brain?
A tap on the head.

What kind of nut sneezes the most?
Cashew!

🍀

What did the electrician's wife say to him when he arrived home at 2a.m.?
Wire you insulate?

🍀

A farmer once crossed a potato with a sponge.
It didn't taste very nice, but boy could it mop up gravy.

🍀

What is brown and sticky?
A stick.

🍀

What is orange and sounds like a parrot?
A carrot.

🍀

Waiter, there is a fly in my soup.
Be quiet, sir, or everyone else will want one too.

What did Old Mother Hubbard say when she went to the cupboard?
OICURMT.

What do you get if you cross a cow and duck?
A cream quacker.

What is aperitif?
French for a set of dentures.

How do you make a sausage roll?
Push it down a hill.

Why did the banana go to the doctor?
Because it wasn't peeling very well.

Where do good turkeys go when they die?
To oven.

Old lady: Can you see me across the street?
Policeman: I'll cross over and if I can see you,
I'll wave to you.

Is it wrong to kiss a nun?
No, as long as you don't get into the habit.

What kind of clothing lasts the longest?
Underwear, because it is never worn out.

Mother: Billy, have you taken a bath?
Billy: Why? Is there one missing?

What was the first mention of tennis in the Bible?
Joseph was serving in the court of Pharoah.

I didn't have any training as a rubbish collector.
I just picked it up as I went along.

Motorist: When I bought this car, you told me it was rust free.
Used car dealer: That is correct sir. I didn't charge you a penny for the rust.

A city schoolteacher took her pupils on a country nature trip.

One of her little charges found a pile of empty milk bottles in a field.

'Look, Miss,' he shouted excitedly, 'I've found a cow's nest'.

Milly: What has a tongue but no teeth, eyes but no ears, and a foot?

Billy: A shoe.

Milly: Bless you.

Have you heard about the couple that met in a revolving door?

They are still going round together.

What bus crossed the Atlantic Ocean?

Columbus.

Wife: I'm worried about my husband, he thinks he's an elevator.
Doctor: I had better have a look at him, send him up.
Wife: I can't—he doesn't stop at this floor.

What vegetable can be used to make dog biscuits?
Collie flour.

I bought a second-hand carpet in mint condition.
It had a hole in the middle.

A fellow arrived at a Luas escalator one night and saw a sign saying DOGS MUST BE CARRIED ON THE ESCALATOR AT ALL TIMES

'Where am I going to get a dog at this hour of the night?' he moaned.

This guy went into a corner shop and said, 'A bottle of sauce please'.
The shop assistant said, 'HP'?
'No', said the guy, 'I'll pay cash'.

I stayed in this hotel and found a dead flea in my bed, so I called the manager.
'A dead flea won't hurt you, sir' he said.
'Maybe not', I retorted, 'but there were several hundred here at the funeral last night'.

She was only a poitin maker's daughter, but I loved her still.

Why did a butcher put sawdust in his sausages?
He couldn't make both ends meat.

What is Beethoven doing at the moment?
Decomposing.

Wife: The car won't start because the engine is flooded.
Husband: Where is the car?
Wife: In the canal.

My husband is a real Do-It-Yourself fan.
Every time I ask him to do something, he says, 'Do it yourself'.

I've been reading a book about helium balloons.
I just can't put it down.

Why do owls not mate when it is raining?
It's too wet to woo.

I've been told that God is a woman.
Great! That means that not alone am I going to hell, but I won't even know why.

A man walked into a bookie's and asked, 'Can I back a horse in here?'
'Certainly, sir,' said the clerk.
'OK Dobbin, back in here.'

How do you know when it is Summer in Ireland?
The rain gets warmer.

Billy: I've lost my dog.
Milly: Why don't you put an advert in the newspaper?
Billy: That would be no good; my dog can't read.

Have you heard about the ship with a cargo of red paint which collided with a ship with a cargo of black paint?
Both crews were marooned.

Milly: Can I try on that dress in the window?
Shopkeeper: Go ahead, it might help business.

Are exits on the way out?

When is a spaceman like a sheet of toilet paper?
When he goes around Uranus and removes the Klingons.

Who invented the five-day week?
Robinson Crusoe. He had all his work done by
Friday.

Is a fellow who rides his bicycle on the
pavement a psychopath?

Have you heard about the sea captain
who set out for India but wound up in the
Mediterranean?
He couldn't tell Madras from Elba.

Shouldn't we call it a swimming ool, as the P is
silent?

We had a brass band at our wedding. It was on
my wife's finger.

🍀

And Saint Patrick said, 'Will all the snakes who wish to remain in Ireland, please raise their right hands'.

🍀

A hotelier boasted that he did not have a single flea on his premises.
It turned out that they were all married with large families.

🍀

To the guy who invented zero—thanks for nothing.

🍀

I am very unfortunate because diarrhoea runs in my jeans.

🍀